W9-ARX-634

Now I Know

Trees

Written by Sharon Gordon
Illustrated by Irene Trivas

Troll Associates

Library of Congress Cataloging in Publication Data

Gordon, Sharon.
   Trees.

   (Now I know)
   Summary: A brief introduction to trees, which,
growing all together, make a forest.
      1. Trees—Juvenile literature.   [1. Trees.
2. Forests and forestry]   I. Trivas, Irene, ill.
II. Title.
QK475.8.G67   1983   582.16   82-20291
ISBN 0-89375-901-5

Take a walk through the woods.

Take a look all around you.

Beautiful trees are all around you!

A tree is a plant.

Like other plants, a tree grows from a seed.

A seed that looks like this...

will grow to be a giant oak tree.

A seed that looks like this...

will grow to be a
beautiful
maple tree.

All trees have roots.

The roots reach deep into the ground.

They "drink" drops of water from the ground.

Then they send the water
up to the trunk of the tree.

A tree trunk makes a good home
for woodpeckers.

A tree is a good place to live!

The leaves need water to make food
for the tree.

Some trees have long thin leaves
that look like needles.

Pine trees and fir trees have needles like this.

These trees stay green all year long.

Many trees have flat, wide leaves.

The oak and maple trees have leaves like this.

These trees usually lose their leaves in autumn.

But before they do,
they give us a beautiful show of color!

Reds and yellows and oranges fill the woods.

In the cold winter, the trees will rest.

Their roots cannot get water from
the frozen ground.

But in the spring, warm rain will reach deep into the ground.

The roots will drink the warm water...

and send new life through the trees.

Then the woods will be filled with
beautiful green trees!